Freak File:
The Unexplained Tales

Gia Scott

DEDICATION

This is dedicated to everyone who ever shared their "freak file" story with me over the years.
You know who you are.

Table of Contents

ACKNOWLEDGMENTS

The years I have spent "collecting" these stories only had any results because of those people who were willing to share their tale with me and their comfort in knowing that the source would forever remain unknown. I have kept that promise, and will continue to do so.

About these Tales

Some of these are things I've seen and experienced. Some of them are not. In each case, these are only the tales I've been told by experiencers whom I believed to be telling the truth. These are not the tales of the mentally ill, those on drugs, or even drunks, but the tales of sober, sensible people just like you and I.

Are they paranormal? Supernatural? Spirits? Demons? Extra-terrestrial Aliens? Secret government operatives?

I don't know. These are the tales of things that a ready explanation with basic investigation could not be found to explain what happened. That doesn't mean they are not explainable, but rather that the experiencer and myself could not explain them.

I'm not a professional paranormal investigator. I'm not sure what a professional in this case really is. I've never heard of anyone but charlatans asking to be paid to do it. I don't pretend to have all of the answers either. I'm merely the collector of stories, and these are the stories I'm sharing with you. None of the experiencers names have been included, as they desired to remain anonymous. I'm not even going to tell you which ones I personally witnessed. Some of these stories may have been told during the course of my radio program, which has also been on the air for a number of years.

If you like talk radio, whether its paranormal or not, you can find out more about my program, Gia Scott's Dawn of Shades, through our Facebook group which is found at www.facebook.com/groups/dawnofshades. Anyone can join, and is normally "approved" within a few hours. The Dawn of Shades is a variety program, and features little straight paranormal anymore, usually focusing on "alternative" topics ranging from permaculture to Native American literature and just about anything in between. It airs live on Tuesday evenings.

Enjoy the stories, and I know you will remember them as you drive down a lonely road in the dead of night, only to have your engine die as mists swirl around and form vague shapes in your dimming headlights. Don't worry, that's not really voices you hear whispering or calling your name in the distance. Dawn will arrive soon now, and you will feel better as the sun rises.

Or will you?

Sit down and listen to these tales and remember, there was always someone left behind to tell the tale. Never mind how many people saw it, at least part way through the event.

Alien Implant

Carol was pregnant with her third child. Her eldest child was going on nine, with the middle one at age seven. A working mother, she was spending a rare weekend morning off pampering herself in the bathroom and shaving her legs when her two daughters came rushing in, excited to tell her about their dreams, unusual because they had both had the same dream.

Just as she was contorting to shave her left leg, the girls got to the part of the tale where they began telling her about the "space ship" that had landed beside their house. At the same moment, Carol found a strange perfect half-sphere lump on her leg. It hadn't been there a few days before, and there was no sign of inflammation as if it had been an ingrown hair.

She half listened to the girls' story as she stared at her leg. Just a few inches from this bizarre lump, a small scoop mark had appeared out of the blue on her shin as well. She was in shock. It was a very bizarre occurrence. Both of her girls were claiming to have dreamed about a space ship landing beside their home and going into it. She had two strange marks appear out of the blue on her leg. Could this just be a coincidence?

She ignored the lump and scar, as though pretending they were not there would make them magically disappear. For several years, she ignored them, and then one day, she gritted her teeth. She would explore this strange lump to see what it was on her own.

She took a razor blade and a deep breath, slicing it deeply through the center. It bled profusely, but there was nothing inside of it.

A few weeks later, she was chatting with someone she

was acquainted with via the internet. Out of the blue, she was told to leave "the thing on her leg" alone. She had never mentioned its presence to anyone, so how could he have known it was there? He told her it was of "no consequence" but that she was to leave it alone, that "they" (implying aliens) knew about it.

So what was it? Did aliens have something to do with it?

We'll never know but over twenty years later, the lump was unchanged. Interestingly, a smaller but otherwise identical one appeared a few inches away. According to doctors, they are nothing more than keloid scars that happen to be perfectly round, resulting from a forgotten injury. None of them believe Carol when she said they both appeared overnight, without a previous injury ever occurring in the area.

Are they related somehow? Are they alien in origin? If so, why?

Alien Voice

This is a very strange tale, but it does not involve aliens as in someone from another country or another world. It's also not about someone or something from another planet. In this case, alien simply refers to just something from outside. In other words, it was source unknown.

Hannah had spent the previous year grieving. She had passed the first anniversary of the death of her son, and while the grief was not gone, she was handling the grief as well as anyone could. That particular night, she was home alone except for her aging mother, asleep in another room. Her husband was out, and it was nearing time for Hannah to go to sleep, as she went to work early in the morning.

She lay in bed, reading a book about pre-Columbian farming. As she put it, "hardly emotionally charged stuff." All of a sudden, she heard a distinct voice, neutral in gender, telling her that she had nothing to live for and may as well kill herself now.

She was stunned.

Even at the very depths of her grieving, suicide had not been something that had crossed her mind. She looked around the room for the source of the sound, knowing that it was not her physical ears that had heard the "voice" in her head. Then, the voice repeated the same message.

"You have nothing left to live for. You are finished. You may as well kill yourself now."

She responded with anger. This was not her thought and no one had the right to "push" thoughts like that into her head.

In response, a series of graphic images showing her that her husband had committed suicide and lay in a puddle of blood. Graphic images of her son's dead body. These images played through quickly, a speedy rendition of her entire family in graphic and gruesome death scenes. Then, the message played one more time in her head, countered by a genuine fury untempered by fear.

With that response, it stopped. There was no explanation for what happened. Hannah insisted that these were not her thoughts, nor were the images born from her imagination.

So where did they come from? What was the actual source?

We'll never know.

Conspiracy theorists claim it could have been the work of some insidious project designed for mind control that happened to fail on Hannah. Was she the victim of such a project? Perhaps. About six months later, her husband attempted to beat her to death, despite no history of violence or physical aggression towards her.

Others claimed that it was the manifestation of evil spirits that were attempting to threaten Hannah, and then resorted to using her husband months later for a second attack.

Hannah shrugs when asked which she thinks it is. She has no idea, and no evidence to support either theory.

Aimee, AIM-mee, aim-MEE...

Back in the 90s, two women were attending a technical college in southern Minnesota. Despite a substantial age difference, they became friends. As the year progressed, the older one had become friends with another student, this one a man, who was between the two women's age. He also developed a serious crush on the younger woman, much to her chagrin, as the trio were friends who spent substantial time together.

The man's crush often encouraged him to drink excessively as he attempted to drown his sorrows. Brian (not his real name) had decided one evening that a few beers and a pool game would be much more entertaining with his two friends in tow, and they agreed to go, although they were not drinking that night. They enjoyed themselves, despite Brian becoming more than a little sappy as he mooned over the younger woman, Aimee. The older one, Zelda (also not her real name) was driving Brian's car, a rather large land yacht type, with electric windows. It was early spring, and a surprisingly balmy night for so early in the year.

Eventually, they convinced Brian that the bar was closing and that breakfast was in order. It was about a 25 mile drive to a 24 hour restaurant, and they made the trip uneventfully. After dumping ample coffee and plenty of food into Brian, they started home down the same highway they had originally taken to the restaurant.

The two women had a long history of playing practical jokes on Brian, trying to shock him and discourage his maudlin behavior over his crush on Aimee. Usually, something peculiar happened to thwart their efforts, but that didn't discourage them from trying. This night was no different.

On the spur of the moment, without consulting Aimee, Zelda took a turn off of the highway, 10-15 miles south of the town where they lived. Driving a mile or two away from the highway, she chose a place to stop the car on a gravel road near the remains of a former farm house. The house and barn was long gone, and the sole reminder that it had once stood there was the patch of native grasses and a pair of trees. Along one side, a narrow creek wandered through the field and passed the homesite, then went under the road in a big culvert. Outside of the trees and dead, matted grasses, everything was barren. They could see empty fields for miles around them.

Both Zelda and Aimee insisted that they had never been there before, that there was absolutely no place for anyone to hide, and that they saw no one there.

The sun wasn't up yet, but it was that pre-dawn glow that illuminated everything. Zelda stopped the car, pocketing the keys. Both of the front windows were down, and Brian rode in the center of the bench seat.

They then started to razz Brian, making him think that they were going to do something terrible to him. Their little game had only gone on for a few minutes when a voice was heard.

"AIM-mee! AIM-mee! Aim-Mee!" it called, the sound originating off of the passenger side where Aimee sat.

Aimee looked at Zelda, who had her mouth hanging open. Both wondered if they had imagined the sound. Zelda's glance shifted to the vacant fields behind Aimee, and she saw nothing out there.

Then, the voice repeated the call, and the spell was broken as Aimee began screaming in terror. Zelda fumbled for the keys, finally found them and started the car, taking off as fast as she could as they put the windows up, just in case. Aimee stared out the back window, worried that something was chasing them but saw nothing.

They got back on the highway and the sun came up over the horizon. Once home, Brian was poured into bed to sleep his night off, and they compared tales. They had both heard it both times, and they agreed—there was no way anyone could have known they were going to be there as Zelda had randomly chosen the country road to turn off on.

Or had she?

Big Foot?

We've all heard stories about Big Foot. But how many times have you been out camping in the wilderness, the wild and wooded areas where Big Foot would really live? This is the story of a skeptic, someone who had no evidence to support the existence of Big Foot, but was willing to leave it as an "unknown" until evidence explaining the things that reliable people saw and heard proves something one way or another.

The story happens in the Florida Panhandle, not exactly a hot spot for Big Foot sightings. Even so, there are miles and miles of woods, numerous streams and ponds, fields and orchards—all of which may provide a food source for a primitive hominid. A group of about a dozen people had been camping in the early spring along one of those small creeks, not far from a larger creek that had water year round. When the weekend was over, the majority of the campers left, heading home for their work week. One couple was left behind, as they intended to camp there for a full ten days.

They were experienced wilderness campers, and this was relatively civilized. There was a gas station and convenience store just under ten miles away. It was also very peaceful and quiet.

Until the sun went down the day after their companions had all departed.

Strange howls were heard, sometimes sounding a bit closer than they would have liked. They had their dogs with them, and the bigger of the two was a veteran of some seriously remote camping trips. When she spent so much time with her hackles raised, softly rumbling as she stared into the darkness, it was eerie. Finally unable to cope with the uneasiness, they retreated to their tent with both dogs.

For about the first two hours, it was quiet. Then, something was repeatedly thrown at the tent, like small twigs and pinecones, making the thin fabric quiver and shake. It went on for hours, and they told themselves they were imagining it, and it was just things falling naturally from the trees. Neither one wanted to recall that their tent was not under a tree.

The next morning, in the bright light of day, their fears seemed silly. There were some twigs and pinecones, but not enough to say yes, someone had been throwing them at the tent. The day was uneventful, filled with typical camping activities such as hiking and bird watching. The evening was quieter too, without the howls of the previous night. Even so, shortly before they had gone to bed in the tent, their dog had begun to repeat her low growling again. She also began to stay exceptionally close to the couple, seldom more than a foot or two away, and flat refusing to let them move behind the tent near the thick undergrowth it backed up to. If either one started to move in that direction, she would simply move in front of them and refuse to move, gently herding them to stay on the front side of their tent.

Exhausted by their restless sleep the night before, they both slept like logs, and if anything odd happened, the dogs did not wake them. The next few days remained peaceful, they had few worries. Then, on the last night, it was every bit as noisy and unsettling as the first night alone in their campsite. Dawn found them awake, and breakfast was made early. A last walk was taken alongside the creek, until the crude path just seemed to vanish in the undergrowth. They turned to head back to camp, it was only about a hundred yards. About halfway back to their campsite, they came to the same branches they had ducked under as they had started out, but this time, they saw clumps of dark hair caught in the bark of the trees.

They were familiar with the common animals to be found in the area. This hair wasn't from a raccoon, white tail deer, or even the less common bears. It wasn't horse hair, and it also was not human hair. It was also on small branches, too small for squirrels or raccoons to even venture out on, all about four and a half feet above the ground.

This was a mystery, but the clock was ticking and a storm was moving in. In the rush to pack up, they forgot all about the hair caught in the branches that they had found. Weeks later, when they returned, there was no sign of the hair.

Was it really Big Foot that had been harassing them at their campsite?

The Black Thing

The Black Thing as it was dubbed, has tales originating all over the world. While each tale differs somewhat, there are some things that indicate that the phenomena is related.

- It is always two or three people who witness it together. (At least the ones who are able to tell the tale.)
- It always occurs near a "UFO hotspot" where people frequently observe UFO type activity and may also deliberately seek to observe it.
- It looked vaguely human in shape, but no features could be seen.
- No matter how the people were traveling, (foot, horseback, bicycles, or motor vehicle) it would always only "almost" catch them.
- The experiencers always experienced an abnormal level of fear to the event.
- The experiencers never wanted to have a repeat experience.

This is some of their tales.

Louisiana

In Louisiana, along the Mississippi border, near the Honey Island Swamp, one couple was on a lonely road with no houses nearby. It was a popular area for watching for UFOs, and it was also their reason for being there that night.

They spotted the Black Thing just out of range of their lights from their car, barely visible. The man, weapon at hand, fired several rounds from a handgun at the creature. It didn't seem to faze it, and it continued to seem threatening, remaining just outside of the lit area. With rising fear, the two jumped into their car and headed towards the main road, with the thing pursuing them. They drove faster, hoping to leave the threat behind, but the man observed it staying just a few yards behind them, as did his wife as she turned around to stare towards it.

It continued its pursuit until they made it all the way to the main highway, after following them down the main blacktop for a couple of miles. Suddenly, it seemed to just vanish, without a trace of where it had gone.

They discussed returning to try and identify it, but the fear had been too intense. Neither one wanted to return without someone knowing what they were doing, where and why.

Oregon

This was a trio, one in her mid-thirties, two in their late teens. The older one and one of the younger were females. They were on a nature walk in an area known for UFO sightings but that wasn't why they were there. It was also late afternoon or early evening, and dusk was just settling in. They had walked along a path through the woods and had emerged into a clearing when the Black Thing appeared at the edge of the woods, from the same side as they had just emerged from.

It terrified them, and they bolted down the path towards the campground where they were staying. The creature, whatever it was, stayed right behind them, forcing them to run as fast as they could. Once again, the level of fear was far more intense than any they had experienced before.

The creature chased them, until the very last bend in the trail before the campground. Then, it just vanished.

Scotland

In this story, there was a pair of teenage boys who had been out riding their bicycles. They had come up on an abandoned quarry, and had stopped for some reason. Once again, it was approaching sunset, and shadows were long and dark. It was another area where UFOs were often seen and reported too.

The two boys were loitering around, for whatever reason is lost in the past. Something moved in the shadows along the edge of the quarry, and they then spotted their first view of the Black Thing. Terror sent them fleeing to their bicycles, with the creature once again pursuing them, just a few yards behind their bicycles.

The two boys rode as hard as they could down the old road that lead to the quarry, with no nearby houses to seek aid and the creature not far behind them. Then, as they approached the edge of the village where they lived, the creature seemed to just vanish into thin air, leaving them feeling a bit foolish.

Once again, the level of fear the two boys felt was abnormal in their opinion. The experience left them shaken, and the level of fear they had experienced left them both uncomfortable spending time with their co-experiencer, effectively ending their friendship.

Arizona

A couple was on their way home from an evening bonfire with some friends, driving down a dirt road that they used frequently, both at night and during the day. It was a ranch road, which meant that there were gates to open and close at several locations. It was also narrow, rutted and unmaintained.

In this case, the man was known for driving excessively fast, frequently in an unsafe manner, something his wife was often chastising him about. She was nagging him about driving too fast when she spotted the thing behind them.

"What the hell is that?" she said, about the same time her husband spotted it in the rearview mirror.

No sooner had the words left her mouth when she had the recurring thought appear in her mind, at the same time as what she called a "primal fear mode" also appeared. The thought was "if it catches me, it's a fate worse than death."

She was soon screaming at her husband to drive faster, as she stared out the rear window at the creature that was pursuing them. The creature appeared to be blacker than the night, without any features she could distinguish. Despite the fact that she knew it was chasing them and that her husband was driving insanely fast on the narrow road, it seemed to be loping along easily, its stride making the pursuit easy. It was as though it was merely playing with them, like a cat with a mouse. Even so, she couldn't think, the fear was blinding, and her husband drove like he was possessed. If one of the gates had been closed, they would have crashed through it, and she was sure later that they had gone around curves on no more than two wheels on several occasions. Just at the point where he had to slow down or they would definitely crash as they approached a T in the road, the creature disappeared, along with the blind panic that had sent them into the headlong flight to escape it.

In silence, they returned home. With their marriage coming apart at the seams, the woman was certain that it was some kind of a sick prank on the part of the man who was soon to become her ex-husband. Embarrassed at being fooled like that, she said nothing for over a year to anyone about what had happened that night. It was only after hearing another experiencer's tale that she was willing to talk about it.

Australia

A couple was out horseback riding and had not returned to the station as early as they had planned for some reason. (The reason has been lost in the retelling.) Sunset was upon them as they made their way home, and they had just passed by a few scraggly small trees. They weren't pushing the horses, it had been a long day and the woman was not an expert rider either.

Suddenly, the horses were obviously spooked, and the man looked around to find the source of their sudden fear as they both attempted to bolt for home. A dark figure, his first glimpse of the Black Thing, appeared near the trees they had just passed. The horses' fear was intense, and now his fear level began to rise as well.

What was this strange thing? Was it some sort of practical joke?

Before long, his fear was turning into blind panic, and the horses' was as well. The woman lost control of her horse first, but the man was soon on their heels. Much to his horror, so was the Black Thing, just a few yards behind him no matter how hard their horses were running.

Then, as they approached the station itself and could see other people near the house, the thing disappeared and their horses began to slow, still snorting and flecked with foam from their fear filled flight. With the horses' blowing hard, the couple's tale was regarded suspiciously, despite their insistence that it was real.

Neither one was willing to ride out into that area until daylight, when further inspection showed no sign of their pursuer.

Had they imagined it? If so, why had the horses become terrified first? What did they really see that evening?

New Mexico

It was late in the evening, and a woman was traveling home with her young son, a seven year old. They were driving down a dirt road the last few miles to where they lived. Suddenly, without warning, something began pursuing them; something the woman only had a brief glimpse of in the rear view mirror. Startled, and assuming it was a dog, she asked her son to turn around and look to see what it was, as she was busy navigating the rutted road. She felt unnaturally fearful of what it was already, which is why she had asked the boy to try and get a better view of what it was.

Terrified, the boy began insisting it was a man who jumped like a kangaroo and he began to beg his mother to drive faster, but then the kangaroo-man seemed to just jump further and faster. For two miles, it pursued them, then as they approached the turn off that would lead them home, it just vanished.

Since it was only about a quarter of a mile from the turn off to their home, and the woman was still terrified, she had told the boy that when they got home, he was to run straight to the door and go inside and not wait for her. They both ran for the door, although the woman was watching all around them as the motion detector lights came on to illuminate the yard. She thought for a moment that she saw the thing across the narrow dirt road from their home, but was not certain. Regardless of whether it was there or not, she spent a terrified night, fearful of something or someone trying to get into the house.

When asked what the kangaroo man looked like, the boy said it was all black, but he couldn't see the face. Like the others, they were in an area with frequent UFO sightings.

Conclusions

The Black Thing is impervious to bullets. It seems to present a threat, although no one knows for certain. The fear is so intense that the fear alone presents a threat because of the physiological reactions to such intense fear. It is also intense enough to prevent anyone from a second encounter. With a broad spectrum of experiencers, it isn't something imagined by anyone—all of these encounters, as well as those not listed here, were independently experienced, all without knowledge of previous encounters.

Only one potential "weapon" has been theorized for the black thing, a thing so black that it seems to have been molded from condensed shadows.

Light.

It flinched from gunfire, not because of bullets, but because of muzzle flash. Light just might be the weapon to keep it at bay. For this reason, many hunters of the weird who roam lonely places at night are now carrying the giant, intense spotlights.

It isn't to find the aliens or to spot deer either. It's for something far more frightening than space aliens, Big Foot, the Loch Ness Monster, or even the Mothman. It's for something no one dares to try and encounter a second time on purpose, a last ditch tool to try and keep this terrifying creature at bay.

It's for the Black Thing.

Bouncing Light Ball

Bethany had had a terrible evening. Her boss had been on her case. Her kids had been unruly and demanding. Customers had had outrageous demands, and it seemed as though the day would never end.

She decided she needed a little break, and a bit of time to truly unwind. So, she decided to buy a single can of beer, then drive out to a local landmark called the "Iron Bridge" that was located high above a canyon down a wide dirt road.

The moon was up, it was about midnight, and she headed out into the country. It was about eight miles from town to her destination, and she would turn off of the highway onto a narrower blacktop road, then follow it for several miles before turning yet again down the dirt road that lead to the iron bridge. The bridge itself was over the end of the canyon, just a few miles before the creek below would dump into a bigger river. Between the bridge and the joining with the river, it would wind past an ancient Indian ruin and the water would spill over a shallow dam. It was an area that Bethany had spent a lot of time in, fishing and camping, as well as hiking, and a favorite spot.

After she had turned down the dirt road, despite laws forbidding it, Bethany opened the can of beer and took a sip as she drove along the roadway. As she got closer to the bridge, hills and curves in the road would obstruct her view of her destination until she was within a mile or so of the bridge.

Just as she reached that point, she could see flickering orange lights ahead. Assuming she was seeing parking lights and was possibly approaching a drug drop, she stopped the truck and turned it around to head back to

22

town, not wanting to get involved in that situation. She had only gone about a half mile towards the blacktop when a small ball of orange light appeared off on the driver's side of the small pickup truck.

Certain it was nothing more than a reflection on the window, Bethany rolled down the window, but the light remained about an arm's length away from the truck, even with the gap between the bed and cab of the truck.

At this point, fear of the unknown began to kick in, and Bethany began speeding up in an attempt to leave the mysterious light behind. It never changed in position, no matter how fast she drove.

Next, she took the beer can, over half full, and threw it out of the window at the mysterious light. Once again, it did not shift position.

She tried swerving and slowing, but that also had no effect. She crossed two metal cattle guards, but it didn't move then either. Nor did it change position as she crossed over a broad creek's reservoir on another metal bridge or the smaller bridge over a narrow canyon. It paced her every move, no matter how fast, as she headed frantically towards town.

As she approached the highway itself, she could see traffic coming, and stopping was unavoidable despite her peculiar pursuer, and she forced herself to slow down despite her increasing fear. As she slowed for the stop sign ahead, several cars were approaching the intersection from the driver's side of the truck, catching her attention as she gauged how long she would have to be at an actual stop at the sign. She was about a hundred yards from the stop itself at that point, and when she glanced towards the location where the light had been, it was moving away from her, remaining at about the same height as it seemed to nearly drift towards a county maintenance yard.

She didn't care. She hurried back into town and home, and suddenly, life and her job didn't look so bad. She also stopped a long time habit of hers of spending long hours alone in the area around the iron bridge, and refused to be in the region after dark alone at all.

What was the light pursuing her?

Her description was that it was amber colored light, slightly larger than a soft ball. Unlike a traditional bulb, it was evenly illuminated without a central brighter point. It was a soft glow, almost fuzzy, with no definable borders as though it was encased inside glass or plastic. She was adamant that it was not ball lightning, that she had seen ball lightning, and it would have never crossed the cattle guards and bypassed jumping to the fence if it had been, let alone crossed the iron bridges without jumping to the rails there. She was firm in that it did not resemble any technology she had ever seen, and that she had no idea what it could have been.

So what chased her that night? Was it a ghost?

Creepy Customer

Every now and again, we all encounter total creeps as we go through both our personal and professional lives. Now and again, something is creepier than usual and you never forget the experience. This is the tale of one such customer, a man in search of a motel room in a small town in the wee hours of the night.

The town was just off of the interstate, so a late night customer was not unusual. After all, that was why she was hired to work the graveyard shift and do the paperwork then. Often, she would rent more rooms between midnight and dawn than were rented before midnight.

She saw the car come down the street, unusually desolate that particular night. Unlike most customers, he parked the car across the street in a small strip mall's vacant parking lot. It was a huge land yacht, old but maintained as though it was new.

She watched the man get out. He was tall and apparently slender in build as he had a narrower silhouette than most men. He also wore a hat, the likes of which had been uncommon since the 1950s in this part of the Southwest. He wore a long dress coat, reminding her of a trench coat, although his was as black as his hat and his car.

Something about him seemed odd as he crossed the street, and while she couldn't put her finger on it even later, it started the creepy feeling and sent her fleeing behind the counter. When the man walked through the door, the feeling intensified until she was sure he was about to try to rob her. Terrified, she had no desire to die for less than the hundred dollars a thief would get. Fearful and unable to find a safe retreat, she retreated as far as she could.

He asked the price for a single room, and she quoted him the highest price, not the one she had been charging all evening. He asked for a downstairs room, and she claimed that there were only upstairs rooms. She did not want to rent him a room at all, she wanted him to leave.

He smiled at her, there was something odd about his eyes, and he had pale skin with what appeared to be the sheen of some kind of oil, as though he was greased on every inch of skin that was visible to her. Seeming to realize that she wanted him to leave without renting a room, he suddenly gave up and departed, still moving oddly. She didn't even wait for him to get to his car before she locked the door, uncertain that even a locked door would actually prevent his return.

With a previous career in law enforcement, the woman was a trained observer, not only of human behavior but of the minor details of how a person moved and their body language. She insisted after her peculiar experience that everything about this man was wrong, from his facial expressions to the way he walked, as though *he was not human at all*, but masquerading as one. Not having been a believer in alien visitation before, she was now dead certain that aliens were walking among us, trying to masquerade as humans.

Had she become delusional? What did she see?

At least for the decade after this experience, she stated repeatedly that this was the only alien pretending to be human that she had ever seen but she still swore that it was an alien who had tried to rent a room that night, a very malevolent alien who had no good intentions towards humanity as a whole.

Could aliens be walking among us, pretending to be humans?

Digital Camera Anomolies

Ruth was a practical woman, but she was also one who loved electronics. As soon as the first digital cameras came down low enough in price to make owning one practical, she had bought one. It was nothing fancy, with its low resolution photos and minimal internal memory. Even with that, their new digital camera allowed the entire family to begin playing with the photos and the idea of digital photography.

At first, nothing odd happened. That was about to end though.

First of all, one of Ruth's sons died. Still a child, the loss and her grief were immense. Perhaps this grief provided the trigger that began the peculiarities.

The camera began producing phantom images, but only when Ruth was in the photograph. At first, she blamed the misty figures on tricks of the light or a camera flaw. They appeared anywhere the camera was used, whether it was an outdoor scene where she was in the photo or if it was a candid shot taken indoors.

Then, it started to happen when other people snapped a photo of her with their digital cameras too. This increased her uneasiness, with the frequency of these misty phantoms.

The last straw occurred at home. She had been rolling out cookie dough to make cookies when her husband snapped a shot of her. Much to her horror, a few minutes later he calls her to the computer. There, instead of her, was someone with long black hair and a large, distinct red feather hanging downwards on one side of her head.

Ruth had brown hair, and didn't wear feathers, whether red or any other color. She also had a well formed face, instead of this rather melted looking one that appeared in the photo.

Ruth banned everyone from using a digital camera to photograph her for a number of years, finally relenting as resolution increased and the use of film cameras began to wane. The photos were normal then, without misty figures or ghostly orbs appearing.

What had been going on while she was grieving intensely? Were the images a message from beyond?

Evil Husband

Hannah and Adam hadn't been married very long. Just over a year. It was Hannah's first marriage, and Adam's second. Most people that saw the couple swore they were the happiest couple they had ever seen, and would readily say so.

They say that looks can be deceiving, and that was true here too. Things were not as idyllic as they appeared on the outside.

Adam's temper was beginning to flare often, and especially if he was denied something he wanted or was contradicted. While Alice was not afraid of the temper, she was afraid of the phenomena that began to appear whenever Adam was thwarted in his latest scheme.

This incredibly foul stench would appear in the air, one so horrible that Hannah would gag.

At first, she told herself that she was imagining it. Adam could never smell it, or at least refused to admit that he could.

Then, the stench began to appear when Adam would return home after one of his late night wanderings, after Hannah had gone to bed. Sound asleep when he would return home and go to bed, she would wake up gagging, ending up sleeping on the sofa for the remainder of the night because of the foul stench that would fill their bedroom.

Fear began to plague her. She wasn't superstitious in general, but this foul stench was not being imagined if it woke her up. She couldn't think of any normal, natural reason that it would appear either.

That only left the stories she had heard as a child about demons and the stench of hell, and she couldn't help but be a bit afraid. Adam was acting progressively more peculiar.

Other people began to notice the foul stench too, if she aggravated him in any way when other people were around. She became somewhat afraid of challenging him, no matter what he had done. He spent money as fast as it came in, leaving them unable to pay bills. Hannah was beside herself, unable to cope with the progressively more weird events that were occurring. Adam had also begun to think of himself as a great prophet, which did not increase her confidence in him.

Adam was a mechanic, and worked on the truck they used, doing some repairs on the brakes, although Hannah had told him that the brakes had not been giving her any trouble at all. After the work was completed, Hannah took the truck to go to work early one morning.

The first time she stepped on the brakes, there was nothing. She pumped the brakes, trying to gain some kind of braking ability, and slowly they began to work at least partially. It seemed that there was air in the lines. That night, when she informed Adam of the brakes' malfunction, she felt a twinge of suspicion about why there had been so much air in the lines.

The next day, while at work, she called and arranged to meet with her insurance agent to change her life insurance policy and retirement benefits in the event of her death. Her husband was removed as her primary beneficiary. If she died, he would get nothing.

Adam had also been pressuring her to change their home's ownership from the family's name to hers, but she had always just "not gotten around to it." Now, there was a gritty resolve in her to avoid doing so, as with the way it was currently set up, he would not receive deed to the property either, should she die.

He had broken her trust, but soon much more would be broken.

Whether madness or demons had caused the problems, it all came to a head one night when Adam had returned from his nocturnal wanderings. They were talking about an issue with the printer and printer paper when suddenly, Adam seemed to lose touch with reality.

He launched himself at her, in a completely unexpected attack. Screaming that she would bow to the prophet, he attempted to choke her. Escaping his grasp, she tried to run for the door, but he was too quick for her. With his right hand on her throat, he began pounding her face with his left hand, even though he was strongly right handed. After a number of blows, Hannah felt the bones in her face creaking from the pressure, and was sure they were about to break, which would surely result in her death.

She played possum, going totally limp.

Adam stepped away from her, seeming to be calmer. With all of the strength and speed she could muster, she scooted away from where he had pinned her, and out the door into the darkness. She could hear him screaming that he was going to kill her, that he was supposed to kill her.

When the police arrived, Adam had been doing peculiar things as though he was hiding something. He had hid their camera under the mattress, along with a number of

Hannah's personal items such as jewelry. The telephone was also hidden, as though to prevent its use.

Later, after being released from jail, he tried to talk Hannah into letting him return to their home. She refused, and the aroma appeared once again. She would not let him return, even with a police escort, instead packing his belongings and having them delivered to him. He swore he had no memory of the incident, and while Hannah agreed that that was possible, she also knew that whatever had possessed him that night to attack her could happen again. He tried desperately to convince her that he really was this great prophet he claimed he was.

Was he just an abusive husband? Or was he actually evil?

Ghost Lights of Tucker Flats

Tucker Flats is a flat expanse of semi-arid land in Northern Arizona, just east of Winslow, Arizona. Located on the west side of Tucker Mesa, it extends both north and south of the mesa itself, with rather indistinct borders.

In this area, "ghost lights" or mysterious bouncing and rapidly traveling balls of light have appeared for decades or longer. Local superstitions have them being everything from evil spirits unable to rest to extraterrestrial beings of some light-being life form. While no one knows for sure what they are, they have long fascinated many people. Often, people will find a convenient perch just to watch the lights moving around on the flats themselves, even bouncing between rock outcrops as they do so.

Tucker Mesa was once-upon-a-time used as a radar base during World War II. After it was decommissioned as a radar station, it was assigned to various agencies, including the Job Corp during the 1960s-1980s sometime. When they departed the rather remote mesa, the buildings were dismantled and used in various other state agencies for other activities. Despite this, a locked gate and armed guard ensures no one gets to the top of the mesa.

Secrecy seems to breed conspiracy theories, and Tucker Mesa is no exception to the rule. There seemed to be a lot of whispers from a wide variety of sources about Tucker Mesa alone, without the ghost lights even. One rumor was that a certain number of young adults who were assigned there during its Job Corp years simply disappeared without a trace, never to be heard from again.

Another one was that these young adults had been put to work finishing the completion of a secret underground base, used for some nefarious purpose. This was furthered by the presence of several vents in odd areas near the mesa. Whether these vents had any purpose or were merely discards littering the desert is unknown, as the security guards would soon swoop down on anyone in the area, whether they were on foot, a vehicle, or horse back.

The oddities didn't stop there. South of the interstate and railroad tracks, the flats continued. Hidden telephone lines and electrical lines were supposedly observed, along with the camps of supposed desert rats who had had a vantage point to observe the goings on at the mesa all contributed to the air of secrecy. It didn't help that these supposed camps were abandoned suddenly, with the food, sleeping gear, and even fuel still left as though the person intended to return, even months later.

The ghost lights preyed on local superstitions and encouraged locals to steer clear of the area, especially at night. One story tells a tale of one local who failed to do so.

The young man was a bit of a daredevil, and had a sand rail or dune buggy. Equipped with the usual safety gear, he was reputed to be not only a good driver, but one who observed safety rules of helmet and safety harness every time he went out, partially because he would take a number of chances that often resulted in the vehicle being rolled over onto its side or top.

One night, he went out to play and wandered onto the

flats, which bordered his usual play area. That night, he didn't return home. He was found dead the next morning in his dune buggy, with it rolled onto its side.

His friends claimed that there was no way he could have been killed in what would have been a minor roll over for him and his frequent stunts.

Freak accident or deliberate sabotage after seeing something he shouldn't have? You decide.

The Golden Armadillo

Even in the natural world, there are times when something that isn't so natural is seen. What are these strange anomalies? Is it a hallucination?

Jacob was coming home after being in town. He lived at a very remote ranch house in northern Arizona, far from power lines and paved roads. It meant a long drive down narrow dirt roads with several gates to open and close. He didn't really mind any of it, including the long slow drive. It allowed him an opportunity to unwind and switch gears between town and the ranch. Today, he had been lucky and able to leave town in plenty of time to make the drive home before sundown, although he knew he would cut it close if he didn't hurry along on the straighter sections of the road.

He was three quarters of the way home and had to slow down as he navigated through some washes and twists in the road. There was some brush on both sides as he ascended through the tight turn up the side of the wash. That was when it appeared.

He slammed on the brakes as it vanished into the brush alongside the road and jumped out of the truck to pursue it.

It had looked like a giant armadillo sort of creature, and in solid gold.

He told himself it was impossible, but he intended to find out what it was.

The tracks were indistinct, either invisible on hard packed soil or rock, or in soft sand that left indistinct smears. He hurried after the creature, tracking it for over a hundred yards. The sun was setting, and he was now out of sight of the truck. It was insane to keep pursuing it now.

What had he seen? Golden ones or not, there were no armadillos in northern Arizona, let alone giant armadillos. It had been just a brief glimpse, but it was distinct in his mind. Somewhat low to the ground, with a long somewhat thick tail that tapered to a thin tip, it had been about three to four feet long, standing about half that high. He had not seen the head clearly, but the body and tail had the appearance of jointed armor, like that of an armadillo.

Had he experienced a hallucination of some kind?

Haunted House

Haunted houses. There are lots of tales of haunted houses, and most towns have an abandoned house or two that is supposed to be haunted, whether or not it is. The "best" haunted houses are large, frequently Victorian or Gothic, two stories (or more) and old. How often does one hear of the haunted ranch style home?

Gary and Mary had bought an old house, but not a really old house. They were only the second owners of the house, despite its age. It was a post-World War II house, build during the housing boom of the late 1940s, and one of many in a new subdivision in a prosperous small town. They had actually purchased it from the estate of the original owners.

Happily they moved in, despite the updating that was needed by the house, and while living in it, began the work to make the house their home. They liked the house, and they liked the neighborhood.

Several family members swore that they saw either the old man or the old woman in the house when they were visiting, but Mary and Gary just shrugged. They hadn't seen anything odd, nor had they experienced anything weird in the house. They were not going to be frightened off by the fanciful tales of family members with too much imagination.

One evening, sitting down with their dinner and a movie, they distinctly heard the door leading to their carport open and then shut, with substantial force. They glanced at each other. No one had a key to the door besides them. Their dogs were both silent, despite the fact that a visitor would have resulted in noisy barking even if they knew them.

Mary went to investigate.

The deadbolt on the door was locked, as was the door knob itself. Opening the solid door, she discovered that the screen door was also hooked. ***There was no way that the door had been opened and someone had gone out.*** It was equally as impossible that someone had come in through the locked door.

They had both heard it, and it had not been their imagination.

What had they heard?

Loon Lake Cemetery

Loon Lake Cemetery is located in Northern Iowa. Supposedly the location of the burial of a number of witches, stories about the place abounded the area. Many people, after an experience in the area, would drive miles out of their way to avoid nearing the cemetery.

One story claimed that if you drove the road that passed near the cemetery late at night that the road would even move or shift in front of you, as though it was trying to cause you to crash, possibly fatally. All of the local stories about the place seemed designed to encourage people to stay far away.

In addition to the stories, there was a caretaker for the old cemetery that lived at the bottom of the hill where it was located. He was a farmer, of the old fashioned sort, with a relatively small acreage and a mixed bag of farming activities. He lived alone, and wore a pair of old-fashioned wire framed glasses that the 70s saw almost return as the latest fashion with John Lennon and John Denver.

A group of college students had been given the task of documenting the old cemetery, from the inscriptions on the stones to anything else that they found there, and the old man was a source of stories to chill their bones and instill plenty of fear. They were careful though, and followed the old man's suggestions about the things they should not do as they did their work. The odd thing was that the old man told them that his job would be done when they were done with their documentation on the cemetery.

They mostly thought of it as an old man's fancy, but

they didn't say anything after their final trip to the cemetery about not coming back. All they said was that it was time for the summer break, and they'd be back after that.

It seems that somehow, the truth was known, for just a week after their departure, a storm hit the area, bringing the tornadoes that everyone feared. It missed the cemetery entirely, but everything was gone from the old man's place except for his mailbox and his glasses, sitting inside. Barn, house, trees, garden, even the livestock had entirely vanished, leaving nothing more than scars where they had been. Even the usual debris field was absent.

Of course, young people also talk to their peers too. The peculiar tale of Loon Lake was told to some of their friends at the college that had sent the original group to the cemetery for historical documentation. They had also repeated the warnings about avoiding certain graves, as well as the supposed curse for meddling with their headstones.

Young people aren't known for a lot of common sense, and they are prone to ample daring. A group of them went to the cemetery again, passing through the now vacant farmyard that had once been the gateway to the cemetery. One warning had forbidden touching a particular headstone, with a statement that said that to do so would result in the person's own death. Another warning had been to never take anything from the cemetery itself, but especially not a headstone.
One pair of the young men couldn't resist, and decided that one headstone would make a perfect prop for their Halloween party, and hoisted it into their van to take home.

Another young woman couldn't resist the dare of touching the forbidden headstone before she left.

Almost to the minute, twenty four hours later, the young woman and another woman were driving to class. The car, for no known reason, went out of control on a perfectly dry, clear day on a straight stretch of highway. It hit a pole, killing the driver, who happened to be the woman who had touched the stone in Loon Lake Cemetery. The other woman, who had been there and had avoided doing any such thing, was unscathed.

That wasn't the end of it, for on the other side of town, the two young men were also hurrying to their classes. A dog ran out in front of them, or so the story goes, and he slammed on his brakes. The tombstone they had stolen from the cemetery still laid in the back of the van, but when he slammed on the brakes, it came flying forward. It killed both men instantly after striking them from behind.

Coincidence? Rural legend? Maybe.

You decide if it's a cautionary tale or a tale of terror.

The Man and his Dog

Katrina was doing dishes late one night. She was fourteen or fifteen years old, and the oldest of four children. Everyone else had gone upstairs to their bedrooms, and she was the last one downstairs. They lived in a big old house originally constructed by the railroad when they had built the town around the turn of the century.

She was nearly finished when she felt someone looking at her, and she spun around uneasily. Across the kitchen, standing in front of the refrigerator on the other side of the table, was a man and a big black dog, like a Labrador retriever.

The man was dressed in timeless clothing, a flannel shirt and jeans. His hair wasn't specific to an era either. Both he and the dog were looking at the girl as if she had just dropped from Mars. She was less enthusiastic about them. While they looked "solid", she instinctively knew that they had not walked in through the back door just a few feet to their side.

She didn't scream either. Instead, she sidled along the stove with her hands behind her to touch the stove and make her way to the other door that lead to the rest of the interior of the house, keeping her gaze fixed on the man and the dog. Their gaze was as fixed on her as hers was on them, but they didn't move a muscle besides turning their heads.

When she got to the other door of the kitchen, she ran upstairs to hide in her bed.

Were they ghosts? Time travelers? What happened that night?

Modern Dinosaurs

The Southwestern American Desert is a place of mysteries. It's a hard place sometimes, but it has sustained life for centuries before technology arrived. Alone in the vast desert, it isn't hard to let your imagination roam to those long ago days before the arrival of Europeans. There are great mysteries there yet. These mysteries can confuse and frighten the observer at times.

Tales abound of creatures that are never listed in any science book, tales as old as time, coming from early settlers and the Native Americans that lived in the region. Feathered serpents, giant hairy men, and magical, mystical creatures all have their place in the tales of the area.

One persistent tale comes from many areas, mostly at lower altitudes. In the Southwestern deserts, the climate is defined first by altitude, and lower altitudes are warmer in winter, hotter in summer, and drier all year long.

The dry riverbeds are typically called "washes", and will usually only contain running water after a storm passes through, often carrying water that fell from the clouds many miles away. A few will also have springs in them, providing a small amount of water to the wildlife that manages to survive in the harsh environment.

When it is dry, many locals use these dry riverbeds as nature-built roads. One of the best sightings of these modern day dinosaurs occurred there.

A couple was traveling in a Jeep through one of these remote washes at the bottom of a canyon one early spring day. It wasn't hot yet, with midday temperatures hovering in the low 90s. It was just at midday when they were making their drive, towards one of the scarce springs in the region.

That was when a pair of what they could only call miniature dinosaurs appeared.

Running on hind legs, standing about knee high, the pair of unknown lizards ran with their tails elevated above the hot sand that formed the canyon's floor. At their peak speed, the couple said the lizards were running in excess of twenty miles per hour, and possibly as fast as thirty miles per hour.

Both were familiar with the desert, spending immense amounts of time traveling around and exploring the mysteries of the Sonoran desert. These lizards had never been seen before, and their shape and manner of movement was also as alien as their size.

Were they really some remnant of the age of dinosaurs? If they were, are the giant snakes and feathered serpents an equally possible occupant of those vast lands?

Navajo Nation UFO Crash

It never made the news, and few people talked about it. The tale is supposed to have originated from two separate sources, neither of which knew of the other one's story.

One was a relatively new arrival to the area that also happened to be infatuated with Native American stories and culture; some claimed it was to the point of being neurotic about it. One night, he came into the house excited, insisting he had seen a UFO that appeared to be on fire, which was on a path to crash somewhere on the Navajo Reservation. Without much credibility as a source, and no one took his insisting that it was true particularly seriously, nor even seriously enough to even make a drive to see if evidence could be found.

A few weeks later, a middle aged woman from a fairly remote area on the reservation happened to be in town. She began to tell the tale of what she had seen, despite English being a second language that she was not particularly fluent in.

Her story was that late one night; something had crashed near their community. Thinking it was an airplane and that someone might be injured and need help, most of the community turned out and headed towards where the craft had crashed. Sure enough, something had crashed but it didn't seem to be an airplane. The strange part of the story was her insisting that something that "sparkled" like "little stars" was in the air and that they had all breathed it in.

She also said that there had been jets following the

thing that had crashed, and that they had zoomed off after the big explosion when the thing had crashed into the side of a small mesa. With the locals milling around the crash site, not much time had lapsed before a number of unmarked government trucks appeared, along with officials of some kind who began asking questions and then threatening the people who were there, telling them that terrible things would happen if they talked about it. Fearful of government agents, the local population soon drifted homeward.

That wasn't the end of the tale though.

She had no idea what the government people did at that first crash site, just that they had been told to not talk about it. Two weeks later, a second mysterious craft crashed within a half mile of the original one. Less accessible, the government vehicles arrived before the locals could approach. All they saw was the debris from a distance, along with more "sparkly stuff" in the air.

She couldn't express exactly what the sparkly stuff was due to her lack of vocabulary in English. It could have been a glowing gas of some sort, but it also could have been some kind of fluorescing powder distributed in the air.

What was it? Was it an experimental aircraft of some sort? Or was it the "space ship" she claimed it was?

Private Eye?

This story stars a young woman, about twenty years old. She had recently had some highly peculiar experiences, and felt especially vulnerable, emotionally, physically, and financially. It was at this point that she was approached by a private investigator she was slightly acquainted with but who should have known nothing about her recent experiences.

The private investigator had a new investigations agency after recently leaving employment with a state government agency. While she was uncertain what the circumstances of his departure actually were, there were a few whispers of misconduct having been discovered that had forced him to depart.

For some reason, he targeted the young woman, who we will call Betty, and began inquiring about some of the specifics of two separate incidents in which Betty had been involved. Neither incident was one in which police reports or other public documents were filed which indicated that Betty had been present, nor that she had had any involvement in the bizarre activities. Both of these were incidents that involved "other-worldly" types of activities that many people believed involved either secret government ops or extra-terrestrial aliens.

He asked questions, questions that made her uncomfortable because they were specific and directed towards extracting information that she had not shared with anyone, not even her closest associates, because of the fearful reactions she endured due to the often vague memories. He persisted, over a period of months, despite denial or claims of no memory of such an event from Betty.

He finally began badgering her about being regressed in a hypnotic session, claiming it would enable her to regain blocked memories. Betty pretended to be considering it, while making herself completely unavailable for continued contact with this aggravating private eye.

Over a period of two years, he badgered her to consent to the interviews and hypnosis, despite the woman's refusal to consider it. He tried all kinds of techniques to get her to agree, from appealing to her that it was her "patriotic duty" to claiming it would result in "justice." Betty hadn't hired him to find anyone or anything for her, and as far as she knew, no one involved would have hired a private eye to inquire about the incidents.

Or would they have attempted to do so in order to find out how much memory of the events she actually retained? During this entire period of time, Betty became increasingly fearful of speaking about the incidents she had been privy to, as low level harassment kept her edgy. She frequently had prowlers near her remote rural home, found drugs planted inside of her home after a trip to town, had her dog disappear, and saw mysterious shapes lurking in the darkness. Was this just the product of an overactive imagination or budding paranoia?

Even a decade later, she would say little about whatever it was that she had seen or observed, let alone what she may have been the victim of, certain that someone or something would retaliate if she did. She eventually was freed from the harassment from the private eye after he moved a couple of hundred miles away, only to die as the result of a suspicious accident.

Was he the victim of his own knowledge?

Old Mary Gibson

Back in the 1960s, a family bought an old house from the estate of a man who then resided in a nursing home. He was very old, and his wife had died over a decade before after a long period as an invalid after breaking her hip in a fall down the cellar stairs.

They hadn't been living in the house very long when the man's son came to ask them for the woman to go visit his father, as he was insisting on talking to her. It wasn't a long drive, only about 40 miles, and so one Saturday, she loaded up the kids and made the drive to the nursing home to see the man.

She had never met him before, and he was not in good health, so she had told her kids to simply wait in the car while she went to see him and see what he wanted to talk to her about. It had turned out that he had a hidden bottle of strychnine hidden in an almost impossible-to-find-spot inside of a cupboard, but he gave the woman very specific directions on where to find it.

Returning home, she got out a ladder to access the cupboard shelf, nearly 8 feet above the floor, where he had said the bottle was. She wasn't particularly surprised to find it—he had been that specific, and had expressed a fear that one of the children of the house would find the poison, resulting in disaster. Recovered, she disposed of the poison, and a few days later, the old man died.

His wife, Old Mary Gibson, had not been known for kindness or consideration of others. Children in town talked of confiscated balls and baleful glares rather than sugar cookies and cold drinks. She had had no friends apparently, and the neighbors had not gotten well acquainted with her despite shared borders for decades. It had not been a house that the children in town would knock on the door on Halloween either. Local pastors had also never called on the housebound woman.

Not long after the incident with the old man, Mr. Gibson, the woman of the house had obtained a Ouija board. With a pair of lady friends, they had played with the Ouija board on several occasions, and had apparently made contact with Old Mary Gibson, as she had been referred to, the woman who had died in the dining room of the house after it had been converted to her sick room after her fall. For the women, it was nothing more than amusement, and the entire experience was forgotten.

Old Mary Gibson apparently had not forgotten so easily. After this, every time the family would be away from the house, whether for a few hours in the evening or overnight, they would return home to find the basement light on, and the chain at the top of the cellar stairs hooked across. The man of the house was certain someone had a key, and changed all of the locks.

It didn't stop, and three locks later, the woman of the house was at the local store with one of the same lady friends that had been with her when they had played with the Ouija board. Encountering another woman, known to her friend, and also named Mary, she looked at the lady of the house and asked if her name was Mary too. The lady of the house replied yes.

The woman went ghostly white and exclaimed in shock, "You are the one that I've been dreaming about. Old Mary Gibson keeps telling me that you need to keep the chain hooked at the top of the stairs. She doesn't want anyone else to fall down them."

Despite months of the light and chain being altered and numerous lock changes, once the chain was habitually latched across the top of the stairs, there were no more incidents of lights being turned on after that.

Was Old Mary Gibson so easily satisfied? Was she judged harshly in her lifetime without just cause or had her nature improved after her death?

Shadow Cat

Tales of "shadow people" abound in the paranormal world, but this isn't about those. This tale is the tale of a shadow cat.

The couple had been spring cleaning, washing windows and curtains, and then rehanging them. Rugs were vacuumed. It was a busy day.

But it was dark now, and their industrious day had come to a close, with the chore pronounced finished. The woman, Iris, had gone into the bedroom and was turning on the television for a quiet hour or two of watching television and reading before going to sleep. As she turned, she saw a black cat jump through the window, moving the curtains out of its way as it came flying down onto the floor and under the bed.

They didn't own a cat and the window that she had just seen it come through was about eight feet off of the ground, with a sheer drop. Thinking a feral cat had come in through the open window somehow, she was aggravated. The window was not supposed to be open, it was early spring and still very cold.

Moving the curtain aside, she was going to close the window. That was when she saw there was a problem.

The window was not open.

Her eyes had told her a cat had come in, open window or not, so she called her husband in to help search the bedroom, especially under the bed where the cat had run to hide.

They never found a cat.

What had happened? Had she just imagined it?
Or was it a shadow cat from some other dimension
that had come to call?

Skinwalkers

The Skinwalkers are a creature from the Navajo Nation, born of black magic, you might say. Through this magic, a person is turned into an animal. These magic shapeshifters then can target an enemy. It is said that if they sprinkle grave dust or the dust of a corpse on their victim, the victim will die. It's also said that if you recognize the shapeshifting magician, and call them by name, they will die.

It starts by the shapeshifter putting on the freshly killed and uncured hide of an animal, the animal which they will appear to be. The victim in this case was Larry and Lisa, who owned property near the Little Colorado River.

There was apparently some dispute over the ownership of the land and the fact that Lisa and Larry didn't want to sell it. It wasn't particularly valuable land, but it was theirs, and it was convenient for work and family. They had a modest home, a pen for a few head of cattle, another for a pig, and one for some chickens too.

The Skinwalkers wanted them to leave. Lisa wasn't thrilled with the idea of naked men wearing uncured hides running around her house at night, full moon or not. Being awakened in the wee hours by screaming men running through her yard, and then dealing with the frightened children afterwards was wearing thin. They weren't Navajo and weren't inclined to give much credence to their belief system or myths either.

Eventually, something had to change. They'd had the sheriff's department out, and they had fired rock salt at their tormentors, but they had still lost three dogs, a cow, and half of their chickens. Tires had been slashed, engines sabotaged, phone lines cut, and windows broken by flung rocks. Desperate, Larry had consulted with some Navajo friends on how to handle their tormentors.

They told him that somewhere on the property, there was a pouch, the equivalent of the physical portion of the curse that had been put on the property. That was not going to be easy to find, as about half of the property was thick brush, with ample thorns for good measure.

It took hours of searching, but eventually, the mysterious packet was found, just a simple cotton drawstring bag with what appeared to be innocuous random objects inside. How could these simple items do anything towards putting an end to the months of harassment and vandalism?

Despite the innocent appearance, the pouch must have had some connection to the problem, because as was predicted, finding it put an end to all of it, granting them peace at home.

Is there something to black magic? Can people really shape shift?

Slimy Visitor

Like the Creepy Customer, this man was also a visitor to the American Southwest, but he arrived on a sunny afternoon in midsummer. He was about to visit a natural landmark, and the ticket taker watched him in the parking lot because he seemed so peculiar.

He too drove a very large and unfamiliar make of car, coal black and while it was obviously vintage (she thought maybe 1970s) it still appeared like new. The man was tall and slender built and wore a long black trench coat and old fashioned men's hat, also in black with a black hat band.

He stood beside the car, and coated his hands and face with some kind of white cream. It was thickly applied, and even from the hundred yards or so between the ticket taker and the parking lot, she could see the smeared cream covering his face and hands. Then, he added black gloves and removed a very large black umbrella from his car, opening it and holding it overhead as though it was raining.

This went from odd to downright weird in the ticket taker's opinion. The American Southwest is a very arid place, with high daytime temperatures even at high altitudes. The cream *might* have been sunscreen, and the clothing *might* be just his poor tastes in attire, but the umbrella pushed it to the downright weird. It wasn't going to rain today, nor was it likely to rain in the coming month.

She watched him steadily as he purchased his ticket and then approached her. He was wearing black gloves by this point, covering his hands. Only his face was visible, smeared with some sort of a white greasy substance. She said nothing about it, merely tearing his ticket and sending him through the turnstile.

Soon, she was rotated away from the gate and into the gift shop for the remainder of the day. She wasn't surprised to see him emerge from the museum and begin to browse, and she had already mentioned him to her co-worker at the register. He bought little, just the usual postcard or two, and paid wearing his gloves still. His umbrella, folded up for indoors, was tucked under his elbow.

One of the tour guides appeared, looking for visitors who might be interested in taking the free guided tour, and said something about the improbability of rain and his umbrella. The look that the man gave the guide was baleful, and made the one who had watched him prepare to enter the visitor center and museum feel a rush of fear. He gave off a wave of malevolence and hatred that was unusual, and she was not a woman prone to flights of fantasy. Shivering, she was glad to see him depart the building, and she watched him walk towards the exit through the window, walking with his now extended umbrella over his head as other visitors avoided him.

She, like the woman who encountered the Creepy Customer, was also certain she had just had an alien encounter of some kind. While she was certain of his alien origins, she admitted that some of his behavior could have been inspired by a number of health conditions that required low to no sun exposure.

Was he really an alien or was he just some poor soul

with more health problems than anything else?

Snow Birds

Snow birds are not really birds at all, at least not in any feathered sense. Snow birds are those traveling senior citizens who head south to escape cold weather and snow, invading the southern tier of the United States by the thousands each fall, only to vanish with the migrating birds in the coming spring.

They are not native to the states where they make their winter homes, and like part time residents throughout the world, they sometimes do things that seem downright stupid to the natives with their unfamiliarity with the region and its hazards.

Arizona is no different. These winter wanderers often find themselves in serious predicaments that exasperate the locals who are put in the position of playing rescuer. A cowboy was on his way home from a trip to town. He had had to go take care of business that day, and had left his wife at home for the day. As he made the trip down the long narrow dirt road that left the highway and began its meandering route to the ranch house, he could see a shiny aluminum trailer in the narrow canyon below him.

Squinting against the harsh desert sun, he groaned. It was an Airstream trailer and he had no idea how the foolish snow bird had managed to get it in there, but he couldn't even get his truck down there from here. He would have to go home and get a horse to ride out and see what he could do about extricating these people from this predicament. His humanitarian effort would cost him the rest of the day and likely into the night as well, and he was not happy with that either. He had work to do.

Harold was not prone to flights of fancy. He was certain that most things could always find a logical explanation. Unlike most cowboys, even in the 1970s when this occurred, he had a college degree. He was far from a fool and was known for being level headed. Returning home, he told his patient wife what the snow birds had managed to do somehow and that he was going to ride out and see if he could help them somehow, if nothing else, rescuing them and taking them to town to call for a tow truck to get their trailer out of the canyon. With that done, he saddled up his horse and rode out. It would take him nearly an hour to get back to the location.

When he arrived, he got a big surprise.

The trailer was gone. There were no vehicle tracks leading in or out of the canyon either. The only evidence that something had been there was a few burn marks in the sand.

What had he seen? Had his mind just been wandering as he drove home and he imagined the trailer there?

Speedy Bird

Birds are incredibly diverse in their shape, colors, flight patterns, and lifestyles. Even so, someone who is familiar with the birds of a region, they can identify them even at a distance, at least as to type. The largest North American bird is the Californian Condor, an endangered species that has been reintroduced into the wild in the Grand Canyon.

Yolanda lived in Northern Arizona, but far from the Grand Canyon. Even so, due to their immense range, she had spotted the condors on a few occasions. She didn't regard herself as a bird watching expert, but she was fairly knowledgeable.

One day, leaving work in a rush and feeling somewhat uneasy, she had started home down a long dirt road. It was a lonely drive, but one that she usually enjoyed as she unwound in familiar territory.

On this particular evening, she spotted a huge bird off to the side of the vehicle, flying parallel to her route, only about ten to fifteen feet above the grade. The bird was really immense, and she estimated its wingspan to be well over ten feet.

At first, she observed it with curiosity. It wasn't a condor, it was even bigger, and no condor could fly at the steady twenty miles per hour at that low altitude in a parallel path. She couldn't get a good look at the head shape, as the sun seemed to glare off of the bird's feathers in a peculiar way. To Yolanda, the bird seemed to be a light brown or gold sort of color. The big wings beat up and down, seemingly effortless as it paced her.

After a mile or so of the bird pacing her at twenty miles an hour and not showing any signs of fatigue or even a desire to soar higher or change its path, fear began to intrude. This bird was not behaving normally or naturally in comparison with known birds, in Yolanda's opinion.

She began increasing her speed, reaching as much as forty five miles per hour, and yet the bird stayed an even fifteen yard distance away, at the same height, and always keeping pace with her. Then, as she approached an area of sharp curves and rocky outcrops, she had to slow down, as well as pay closer attention to the roadway ahead of her.

The bird just disappeared.

She didn't see it in the sky around her, nor spot it on the remainder of the journey.

What had she seen? Was it a real bird? Maybe an early prototype of a drone being tested in a remote area? Did she imagine it?

Texas Truck Stop

A single mother, traveling with her two children, was nearing the Texas-New Mexico border between Amarillo and Tucumcari on Interstate 40. It was long after midnight, and equally as long until dawn at this point, and it was early Sunday morning on Labor Day weekend. Despite the holiday weekend, traffic was light at this time of the night, but Susan (not her real name) still needed gasoline and all three of them needed a bathroom stop. It was 1994.

It wasn't long until a small truck stop, rather old fashioned looking, appeared on the passenger side, right alongside an unlit exit from the interstate. They took the exit, which lead practically directly to the little truck stop. The gas pumps were old, and it was hard to believe they were still in service, decided Susan. They resembled the type that had been in use when she was a kid, in the 1960s. The whole truck stop was nestled down at a lower level than the interstate, which stood up a steep bank beside the truck stop, and there were a number of big old cottonwood trees standing around buildings too. Susan was uneasy, but the need for a bathroom had begun to become urgent, so she shepherded her children into the building.

There were three or four people inside the store, and at least one man and one woman. They stopped what they had been doing and stared at the woman and the two children coming in as though they had never seen humans before. Susan became more uneasy as she noticed that all of them were remarkably similar in appearance, as though they were siblings. Their stares were setting off a million "Mom Alarms" too, and she was uneasy enough that she made both children (a boy and a preteen girl) go into the restroom together with her, despite it being a one toilet-no stall sort of restroom. They each took a turn, facing the wall when it was someone else's turn, and then headed back out into the store.

The restrooms had been located up a short stairway, about 8-10 steps above the store itself. Susan didn't remember seeing anything resembling a café, but she did remember that all of the goods for sale appeared to be decades out of date as she looked at the packaged candy and drinks. With her increasing uneasiness, she bought nothing, including gasoline, and hustled the children out to the car, where they immediately departed.

While a group of oddballs certainly could be working in a remote truck stop in the middle of the night, that wasn't the end of the peculiarities. Because of how out of place the little truck stop had been, they attempted to find it again on future trips through the region.

There was no truck stop of that description between Tucumcari and Amarillo, on either the north or the south side of the interstate. There was no exit that went to a location similar to what they had seen, nestled below the interstate with a handful of large cottonwood trees. As the mystery deepened, so did their attempts to explain away that peculiar night, and they began inquiring with truck drivers who frequented the region on whether or not they knew of such a truck stop.

No one knew of it, and they all insisted there was no such place.

Where did they go that night? Had they traveled back in time? To another dimension?

Some suggested that they had walked into a camouflaged space ship. Was that it? Who were those remarkably similar looking workers inside of that ancient truck stop? Why were the packages all more appropriate for another era, some 30 years before their arrival there? What had they really experienced?

The Warning

Margaret and her husband, Lawrence, were running errands. They were in their late 60s and 70s, but physically doing fairly well. Living independently, Margaret also took care of her aged father, at that time in his 90s, who lived in the old house. Margaret and Lawrence lived in a spacious newer mobile home a couple of hundred yards away.

On this particular day, Margaret's father was on a visit to one of his other children, hundreds of miles away. Neither household had a dog anymore, and the houses were entirely empty with the elderly couple being in town on errands.

The errands had involved trips to two neighboring towns, with their home located just off of their route between the towns. They had completed half of their errands and were headed off to complete the other half. It was then that Margaret remembered she had left a bill she wanted to mail on the table at home. They would pass right past the post office at the second town on their route, making it easy to mail it on its way, so she thought that stopping by home to pick up the forgotten envelope would be a good idea.

Just then, a voice, very distinct and rather loud, told her "Do not go home. Just keep on going."

She questioned it for just a minute, and the message repeated.

Now Margaret wasn't the kind of woman that had otherworldly experiences, but for some reason, she decided that listening to the voice was a good thing to do today, and she didn't slow down as they approached their driveway, continuing on. They wouldn't return home for another two or three hours now.

When they finally did return home, it was to a depressing sight.

Someone had broken into their home, stealing a number of things, but concentrating on a few things—her extensive collection of Native American silver and turquoise jewelry and her husband's antique hand gun, a massive revolver. They had even taken the ammunition for the gun. Their television, china, silverware, and VCR were where they had always been.

The police were called, and the report was filed. The police officer, upon hearing the story of the voice, told them that they were lucky. It appeared that the thief knew what to take and where it was kept, indicating it was someone they knew. If they had walked into the home while the burglary was in progress, especially since a firearm was among the things taken, it was highly probable that they would not have survived the experience.

Who or what had warned Margaret that day?

The Water Tower

Sometimes, there just isn't an explanation that works. This is one of those stories.

Back in the 1970s and earlier, many national forests in the USA had work camps. Like small towns, they housed the mostly men who worked in the forest, doing everything from logging to fire tower watches. Their families also lived there, and many of the camps had a store, school, and even a post office as part of their facilities.

The Apache Sitgreaves National Forest had one of those, located in the northern portion of the national forest. In the 1980s, many of these were dismantled and abandoned. This one was mostly dismantled, with just a small portion of the original camp left behind.

By the late 1990s, it was a memory that had been forgotten by more people than remembered it had been a functional town in the past. Ellen worked with a man who had been raised at the camp, so she had heard some of the history of the camp.

On this particular day, it was early fall. Ellen and her mother, along with her two daughters, had been out in the forest. They had picnicked and taken a few walks, but most of the day had been spent just slowly driving around on the narrow forestry roads.

On the way home, they had the highlight of their day. A baby bear, about half the size of a full grown bear, crossed the narrow road just a car length ahead of them. It was a rare sighting that close, and they were still talking excitedly as they began the climb out of the area they had been spending the day in.

On their route home, the dirt road would go through the remnants of the work camp before joining with the paved highway that would carry them home. As they rounded a sharp curve, they spotted a giant silvery tank that almost seemed to be floating above the high ponderosa pines in the area.

They were all surprised. It was obviously a brand new tank, it was too shiny to be anything other than new. In addition, they all knew that there had been no tank there before. That could only mean one thing: the work camp was going to be re-activated.

The next day, back at work, Ellen had relayed the story to her co-worker that had grown up there who shook his head, telling her that there was no way that the camp was being re-activated. In addition, it made no sense to install such a large water tower.

Ellen and her mother knew what they had seen, and it had been a very large water tower, similar to those round water towers that supplied towns all across America with water. To prove that she had seen it, Ellen decided to make a trip out there once again, on her next weekend.

Once again with her mother in tow, she headed out to take her pictures as proof. There was a problem though. There was no water tower. There was nothing. The trees in the area where the tank would have had to have been located were intact, and there was no room for a water tower to have ever been in that location.

What had they seen?

Some people believe that they saw a UFO hovering over the trees and had passed it by, oblivious to its presence. After all, it wasn't that far to the area in Apache Sitgreaves forest where Travis Walton had been abducted from. Even so, a UFO in broad daylight?

The Water Woman

There are a lot of creepy places in the world, and many tales of terrifying creatures involve a body of water. So does this one.

The site of the incident was a reservoir, most of which was bordered with cliffs, and it was located in the arid Southwest. It wasn't a vast reservoir, but it did provide locals with a place for water based recreational fishing, boating, swimming, canoeing, and even some not-so-legal cliff diving on occasion. The reservoir was reputed to be as much as a hundred feet deep in places, after eons of erosion by wind and flowing water. It was not very wide, but it wound its way through the canyon for miles before becoming too small and narrow for boats to use.

There was a designated swimming area, but unfortunately, the "beach" was usually plagued with an invasive and unpleasant plant known as camel thorn. Equipped with wicked thorns, it was not only painful on feet, but grew tall enough to tear at legs and waists as well. In addition, the swimming area had more mud than sand, and also lacked the attractive rocky features that were found on the opposite side, near the pleasantly landscaped picnic area. Often, local people opted to swim and fish side by side on the deeper side, despite the drop offs and rocks. The original boat launch was also located on that side.

The water was cold, cold enough to have rainbow trout thriving in it. It was also crystal clear except the first day or two after a heavy rain, which wasn't that often. The views were amazing, with the reds and tans of the rock cliffs contrasting with the stark blue of the sky and the deep blue-green of the water. Willow trees, sage brush, and cattails clung to the edges of the water wherever they could get a foothold, adding more color and texture to the scenery.

Drowning was also common there, with one or two people falling victim to the water every year, whether due to accidents or alcohol/drugs influencing their judgment. On this particular day, a young boy named Johnny was swimming alongside the old boat launch, his family nearby and his parents keeping a close eye on him. He was eight years old, and his younger sisters played close to his parents' side. Several aunts, uncles, and cousins also were in the water, with the adults all being vigilant to prevent any mishaps with the children.

Without warning, and seemingly without even moving, Johnny was pulled underwater. His parents and other relatives sprang into action to rescue him. There was a frantic few minutes of searching underwater without success before suddenly, his body floated upward just a few feet from his searching mother, who frantically dragged her son's limp body to the shore.

Johnny was quickly revived, but his family still took him to the hospital, fearful of damage from the boy's time underwater. The strangest part was the boy's story.

He claimed that a woman had grabbed him and pulled him underwater, and had wanted to keep him there with her. She had been frightening to the young boy, who wanted his own mother. Even so, the underwater woman had intended to keep him. He gave a very clear description of her as well—she had long white hair and had very pale skin, as well as a white dress on. Her eyes were as blue as the sky too, and she had long fingernails, as white as her hair.

Until she saw his real mother searching for him.

The mother's fear and frantic search forced her to let the boy go, and that was when he had begun to float upward towards the surface.

What had he seen? Was it just the product of oxygen deprivation?

His family had to wonder. The boy had long scratches on both legs and both arms, exactly where the woman under the water was supposed to have grabbed him to pull him towards her lair, as well as where she had held him while she tried to convince him to stay with her. Had they just come from a rocky outcrop under the water?

ABOUT THE AUTHOR

Gia Scott was born, just like everyone else, but she also was born to a family that included politicians, used car dealers, and horse traders. Along with that illustrious lineage, she was related to vaudeville performers, horse trainers, cowboys, entrepreneurs, teachers, and preachers. There is also a liberal seasoning of family fruitcakes hidden in her family tree, and some have claimed that someday, Gia will join that list if she isn't more cautious.

With such diversity surrounding her from childhood, she still managed to grow up and develop a deep love of books. It was only natural that along the way, she would write them too. The Survivors: The Time of Chaos is her first published novel. She has also written a collection of true from life stories entitled Freak Files: The Unexplained Tales. Along a more practical train of thought, she also wrote Being Prepared Without Being A Kook, an emergency preparation guide.

After decades of experimental cooking, much to her family's chagrin (after all, the family is inflicted with the less-than-wonderful versions that never see print!) Gia began writing food articles and a food blog. It was inevitable that cookbooks would follow. This is the tenth cookbook. Previous titles include: All Chocolate—Easy & Economical Recipes Anyone Can Make At Home, 55 Fantastic Fudges, The All American Biscuit, 56+ Marvelous Homemade Mixes, 55 Frightfully Fun Foods, A Home Style Thanksgiving, At Grandma's Stove, The Poverty Perspective: Recipes for Rock Bottom Budgets, Fruitcake! and My Precious Cookbook.

Today, after many incarnations along the way, Gia Scott

lives in Mississippi with her husband, three dogs, and two cats in a funny little house surrounded by very big and gnarly trees. Having reached that age of privilege, she can often be found in her garden, wearing peculiar clothes and tending her plants. When she can talk her husband into it, they enjoy going for road trips, looking for the elusive town of New Hope. In between road trips and gardening, she manages to fit in an internet radio talk show called the Dawn of Shades, interviewing a variety of people, including other authors, and promoting causes dear to her heart.

In addition to all of that, she still maintains blogs on general topics, cooking & food, and camping, emergency preparedness & outdoors activities. She also helps with content for websites.

Links

Gia's other books can be found at http://bit.ly/GiaBooks

Gia's general blog is found at www.giascott.wordpress.com.

Gia's food blog is found at
www.gulfcoastfoods.wordpress.com.

Gia's camping blog is found at
www.getreadygo.wordpress.com.

Her website is found at www.exogenynetwork.com

Her author page on Facebook is found at
www.facebook.com/giascottblogs

The group page for Gia's radio program is found at
www.facebook.com/groups/dawnofshades

www.ingramcontent.com/pod-product-compliance
Lightning Source LLC
Chambersburg PA
CBHW050421290526
45786CB00003B/1356